Teaching Children to Write

The Process Approach to Writing for Literacy

Pam Hodson and Deborah Jones

David Fulton Publishers
London

David Fulton Publishers Ltd
Ormond House, 26–27 Boswell Street, London WC1N 3JZ

www.fultonpublishers.co.uk

First Published in Great Britain by David Fulton Publishers 2001

British Library Cataloguing in Publication Data
A catalogue record for this book is available from the British Library

ISBN 1–85346–754–5

The publishers would like to thank Rosemary Appleyard for copy-editing and Sophie Cox for proofreading this book.

Typeset by Mark Heslington, Scarborough, North Yorkshire
Printed in Great Britain by Bell & Bain Ltd, Glasgow

Contents

Acknowledgements   v

Introduction   vii

How to use this book   ix

Chapter 1   The process approach to writing   **1**

Chapter 2   Writing narrative   **22**

Chapter 3   Writing poetry   **40**

Chapter 4   Writing non-fiction   **53**

Bibliography   85

Index   87

For our parents:
Brenda and Lennard Jones
and to the memory of Ron and Sheila Hodson.

Acknowledgements

We would like to thank teachers and children in the London Borough of Richmond where this book originated, especially to former colleagues in the English department at Shene School and in the Richmond Inspection and Advisory Service. In addition we should like to acknowledge the support of the many people who have been involved in the development of this book: Peter Doyle-Smith, Therese McNulty, Paul Davison, Donna Collins and staff and students at the School of Education, Brunel University.

Introduction

In the twenty-first century methods of communication are evolving rapidly. Writing, however, still continues to play a vital role in both our public and private lives. It is a tool which may be used for good or ill, as a means of self-expression or of manipulation. Skilful writers are empowered members of society and have the ability to influence the world around them. Therefore, the effective teaching of writing is fundamental to creating successful and confident individuals who are equipped to meet the demands of the world in which they live.

Recent inspection reports carried out by OFSTED, however, present a depressing picture of how writing is taught in the majority of primary schools. Children's writing is described as 'brief and fragmentary', often incomplete and 'lacking a clear sense of purpose'. Within the context of the National Literacy Strategy, teachers are described as being more confident in teaching reading and as a result, spend less time on teaching writing. In addition, evidence from SATs results show, 'standards of writing lagging considerably behind standards of reading'. In order to remedy this, it is recommended that teachers should plan a coherent and sustained approach to the teaching of writing. Children need to become familiar with different types of text, both fiction and non-fiction and also need to develop an awareness of how considerations of audience and purpose affect writing. Adopting a process approach where the different stages of 'planning, drafting, revising and proof reading' are used, is highlighted by OFSTED as another strategy for improving standards.

The process approach to writing assumes a particular view of how children learn, how teachers teach and of how classrooms function. It allows children to experiment with language, and to develop an understanding of how writing works within an environment where collaboration is welcomed, and independence encouraged. In this context children become confident writers, secure in the knowledge that teachers will give a supportive response as they take risks and make hypotheses about the writing system.

Having identified these issues, the key question arises of how the process approach can be implemented in the classroom. This book is, in essence, a book about the teaching of writing. It aims to explain and build upon the approach recommended by the English National Curriculum and the National Literacy Strategy and to provide structures which enable teachers to introduce appropriate strategies into their classrooms.

The process approach rationalises the decisions children have to make in creating their text, for example, a brainstorm will allow them to record relevant details without having to think about form, accuracy or presentation. In this way the writing is broken down into different stages so that it becomes manageable, giving children increasing control over their work. It also enables them to craft their writing and change it. As they progress into the drafting stages of their work, writing frames, along with the support of adults and peers, provide the scaffolds to enable children to develop their writing successfully.

In using this approach, teachers will seek to promote independence in children, allowing opportunities for more focussed individual and group work. It also allows the teacher to intervene effectively at key stages in the process where drafts and completed frames provide clear evidence of children's writing development. The process approach provides teachers with coherent structures that can be modelled with the pupils themselves.

The book balances rationale and research with practical ideas for teaching writing in the classroom context. These practical ideas include writing frames offered at each stage to support children as they experiment with many different forms of writing, both fiction and non-fiction. They provide a structure and direction for children's ideas on a chosen topic and act as a scaffold to support the writer. At this point we need to make the distinction between writing frames and prompt sheets. Both are designed to encourage informed dialogue between teachers and children and children and their peers. The prompt sheets, however, rather than presenting a structure in which children can write, provide questions which help them reflect on and develop their writing. The fundamental purpose of these frames and prompts is to encourage children to be independent writers.

How to use this book

The frames have been designed for immediate use by individual children. However, from a practical point of view, teachers may find it helpful to enlarge the frames to A3 size to facilitate whole class or group teaching and children may also benefit from the enlarged size as they engage in paired or collaborative group work. Another way of using the frames is to transfer then onto acetates and use the overhead projector to aid the modelling process. The frames have been designed to match the structures of specific genres, but are flexible enough for teachers to adapt them to fit in to a particular topic in a variety of different ways.

Chapter 1 lays the foundations for the general approach to the teaching of writing which is adopted throughout the book and makes the different stages of the process explicit. Many of the figures used in this chapter are generic and can be used selectively across a range of genres. Chapters 2 and 3 explore narrative and poetry and aim to develop children's writing skills in these particular areas. Chapter 4, 'Writing non-fiction', is sub-divided into the different categories of: recount, report, instruction, explanation, persuasion and discussion. It provides structures which enable children to gain a secure understanding of the different ways of writing non-fiction.

This book originated in response to teachers' needs and has been used successfully in both primary and secondary phases. We hope that it will continue to evolve as teachers and children work together in the process of crafting writing.

1 The process approach to writing

In a process approach . . . writing is more than the simple eliciting of a product by the teacher; it is a process that involves thinking and shaping meaning. . . . A process approach views children as authors and treats their written work as creative and meaningful.

(Graham and Kelly, 1998)

At the heart of the process approach to writing is the belief that the stages children work through are as important as the final, completed text. Becoming an accomplished writer involves understanding what each of these stages entails and creating a text certainly means more than 'one shot writing'. This chapter describes the discrete stages of this approach and explains how children can be supported at each stage of their writing journey (see Figure 1.1 below).

Children may go through all of these stages when composing a piece of writing, but as they gain more confidence, they may decide that not all of them

- Making decisions
- Planning:
    Brainstorming
    Organising/Grouping
    Using flow diagrams
- Drafting
- Responding
- Presenting and publishing
- Reflecting

Figure 1.1   The process approach to writing

are necessary. Children, however, do need to have all of the stages made explicit to them in order to give them the necessary knowledge and understanding of how writing is constructed so that they can make informed decisions later and choose which elements they need at different times.

Current initiatives in the teaching of literacy recognise the significance of the process approach to writing. The English National Curriculum (1999) states that at Key Stage 1, children should 'assemble and develop ideas on paper and screen [and] plan and review their writing, discussing the quality of what is written'. At Key Stage 2, children should 'use the planning, drafting and editing process to improve their work and to sustain their fiction and non-fiction writing'. In addition, The National Literacy Strategy (1998) acknowledges that 'through Key Stage 2, there is a progressive emphasis on the skills of planning, drafting, revising, proof reading and the presentation of writing'. Both major initiatives then, clearly identify the need for children to be taught the process approach to writing.

Making decisions

> Children learn through making decisions. They search their lives and interests, make a choice and write. . . . They learn to control a subject, limit it, persuade, sequence information, change their language . . . all to satisfy their own voices, not the voices of others.
>
> (Graves, 1983)

Teachers need to give children as much autonomy over the writing process as possible, by offering them opportunities to choose their own topics for writing. If they always have to write on a subject chosen by the teacher, frustration or boredom may occur, but when children have control over topics this not only increases their enjoyment, but it also contributes to their sense of ownership.

It is important that children are aware of the decisions that will affect the writing they are about to undertake. So they need to have a clear sense of the following: the audience, (who the writing is for); the purpose, (the reason why they are writing); and the form, (the type of writing that is most appropriate to this particular task – see Figures 1.2 and 1.3). Clearly, explicit considerations of purpose and audience will affect the type of writing that children choose. Teachers can develop children's understandings by focusing on these aspects within shared reading and writing sessions. There are obviously strong links between the breadth of children's reading and the variety and appropriacy of the writing they are able to produce. Both shared and personal reading is an essential part of the process for children. With the guidance and support of the teacher children need to be exposed to different models of writing and to explore a variety of text types from the train ticket to the novel. This knowledge will then feed into their own writing and inform not only their decision making, but also the ways in which they go about crafting their own texts. Children, therefore, need the necessary understanding of how texts work in order to make informed decisions about their own writing.

Writing record

Topic	Audience Who am I writing for?	Purpose Why am I writing?	Form What type of writing should I use?

Figure 1.2 Writing record

Making decisions

What do I want to write about?
Who will read my writing?
Why am I writing this?
What type of writing will I use?

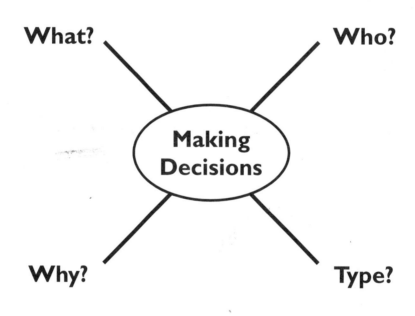

Figure 1.3   Making decisions

Planning

> Plans . . . are powerful devices which can contain dense information yet can be seen at a glance by the writer, whose mind is then free to engage in the detail of composition, referring to the overall direction when necessary.
>
> (Parker, 1993)

There are many ways in which children can organise their thoughts and ideas. Giving them strategies to do this is a vital part of the process which will not necessarily be obvious to them. In this section, we will be focusing on three main strategies: brainstorming, grouping and using flow diagrams.

Brainstorming

Having decided upon the topic, children need to think about the potential that it holds. Brainstorming provides children with the opportunity to record as many initial ideas as they can, whether in a written or pictorial form (see Figure 1.4). At this stage, children need not be concerned with issues such as correctness of spelling, punctuation or grammar, and are completely free from restraints of structure and organisation. A brainstorm is essentially written by the child for the child.

Organising/grouping

Figure 1.5 can be used to assist children in categorising the ideas from the brainstorm under relevant headings or themes. It is important to remember and emphasise to the children that not all topic areas included in the brainstorm need to be used at this stage. Some may be too far removed from the focus of the topic, while attempting to include all of them may result in a superficial piece of writing. These decisions will make for useful points of discussion between teachers and pupils and, as many children find this aspect of planning particularly challenging, it is essential that the teacher models this process clearly.

Using flow diagrams

The next stage focuses on sequencing these ideas in an appropriate order which will provide the structure for the writing itself (see Figure 1.6). Teachers' interventions will be invaluable at this point as they discuss these aspects with pupils. There are key issues which children need to reflect on in order to help them structure their writing. A simple narrative or story, for example, will be structured according to time (chronological), whereas a piece of writing which focuses on a topic, such as dinosaurs, may be structured non-chronologically.

These activities act as scaffolds, supportive strategies which allow the children to both reflect on and craft their writing from the earliest stages.

Brainstorm

Write down all sorts of words of phrases you can think of that have something to do with your writing.

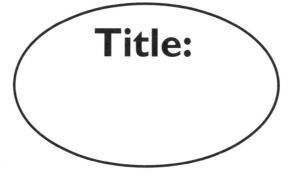

Title:

Figure 1.4 Brainstorm

Grouping

Put your brainstorm words or phrases into groups (look for similar ideas).

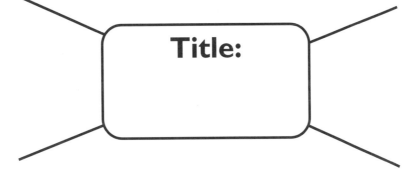

Title:

Figure 1.5 Grouping

Flow diagrams

Now put your groups into order.

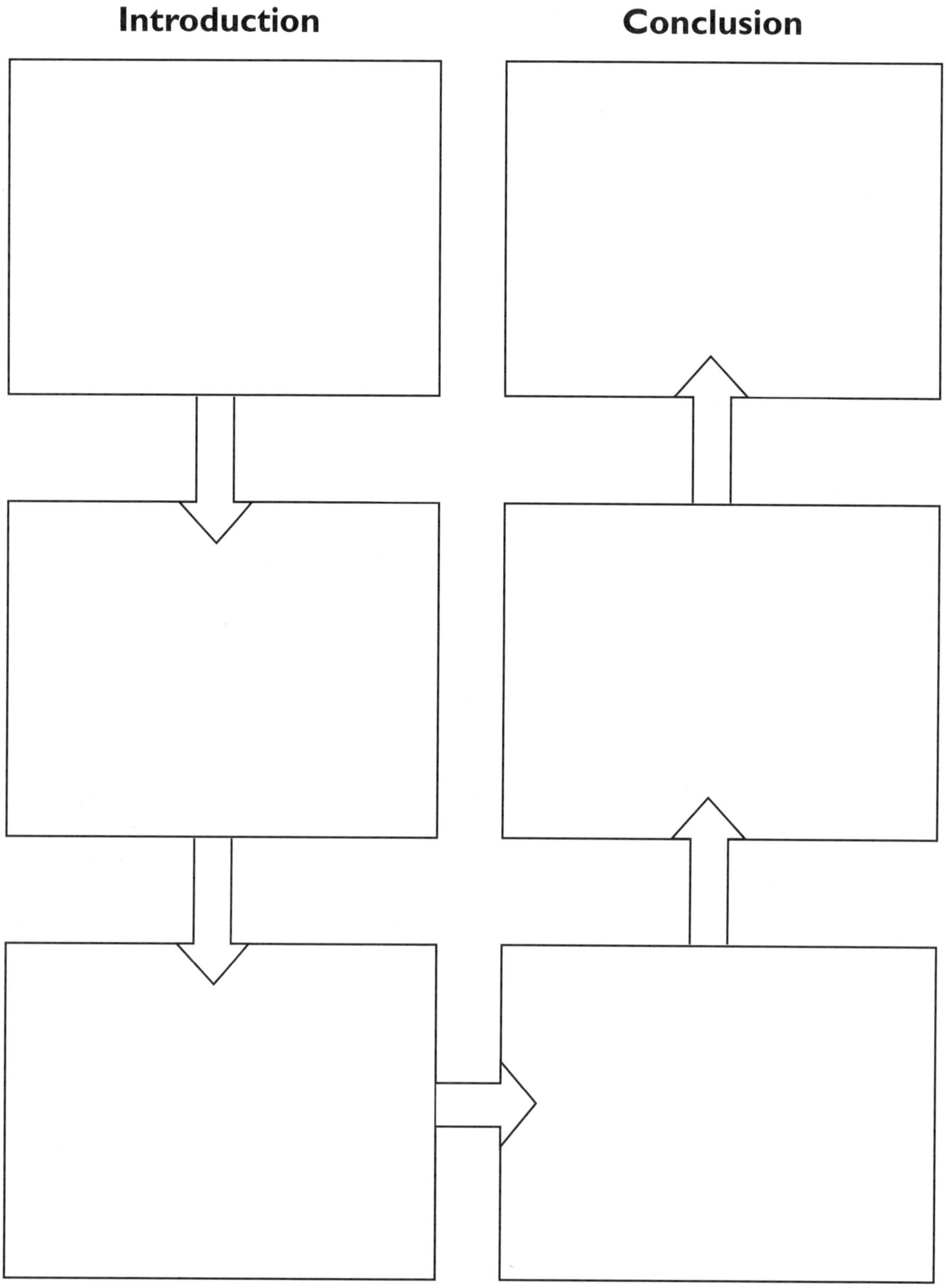

Introduction   **Conclusion**

Figure 1.6   Flow diagrams

© Pam Hodson and Deborah Jones (2001) *Teaching Children to Write*. London: David Fulton Publishers.

Drafting

> One of the best kept secrets in school . . . is that most professional writers produce draft after draft; that they attack what they write, erasing, adding, altering, and moving words around; that they rarely write on just one piece of paper at a time . . .
>
> (Smith, 1982)

This 'secret' is one that should be shared with children. Teachers need to show children examples of different writers' drafts, to write for them and with them, changing, eradicating and inserting different parts of the text. It is in this way that children learn that mistakes and amendments are, in fact, legitimate, and a natural part of what it means to be a writer. The success of using the process approach to writing is largely based on the idea that children are writing as real writers would and can work through successive drafts if necessary.

First draft

It is important to make children aware that the purpose of the first draft is to use the ideas outlined in their flow diagram to begin composing their writing. At this stage, children should not feel the constraints of transcription issues such as spelling and punctuation. They need to know that these will be addressed after the second draft. Figure 1.7 reminds children of these points and reassures them as they begin the process of drafting. It may be helpful for children to use the drafting code "Reading for Meaning" (Figure 1.8), as a prompt either during or at the end of their writing. Having a code which is shared and understood by all children is a helpful tool for collaborative writing in general.

Second draft

As children approach their second draft, they need to be encouraged to reflect more explicitly on meaning, appropriacy and clarity. In Figure 1.9, they are presented with questions and prompts which enable them to do this, and discussions with their response partners should focus attention on the issues raised here. Not only should children look at the structure of a text as a whole, but they should also consider specific areas such as relevant choice of vocabulary, length and variety of sentences and the use of connectives. At this point, as with others, all these aspects should be viewed in relation to audience, purpose and form and the ways in which they contribute to the overall impact of the writing.

Once children have reviewed their writing with a focus on meaning, transcriptional issues such as spelling and punctuation need to be addressed. As with Figure 1.8, Figure 1.10 offers children symbols that they can use to annotate their own text. Attention should also be drawn to the fact that they can draw upon a range of support structures, for example, dictionaries, computer spell checks and response partners and that a systematic use of these strategies can help them produce more refined texts.

First draft

Using your flow diagram – write out your first draft. Remember: audience, purpose and form.

Now it's important to concentrate on what you want to say.
This draft is for you – you may cross out words, or leave gaps.

(Don't worry too much about your spelling and handwriting – you will be going back to this later.)

The most important thing now is to concentrate on meaning.

Figure 1.7 First draft

Reading for meaning

You can use this after or during your first draft.

Cross out

Something left out

Change, make clearer

Move text around

Action:
See your response partner

Figure 1.8 Reading for meaning

Second draft

Read through your first draft.

Think about the person who will read it.
Does it make sense?
You might like to read it aloud to your friend
– listen to their comments.

Is there anything you want to add at this stage?
It might be just another word, a whole sentence,
or even a whole paragraph.

Is there anything you want to cross out – a word,
a group of words, or a whole paragraph?

Are your ideas in the right order?
You can change them if you want to.

Figure 1.9 Second draft

Reading for mistakes

You can use this after your second draft.

Spelling:

Punctuation:

Action:

Use a response partner/

a dictionary/an adult

Figure 1.10 Reading for mistakes

The aim is to give children as much autonomy as possible during the drafting process. It is perfectly legitimate for them to develop their own notation for changing and developing the text, although shared codes promote a shared response from both peers and adults. The use of ICT in this is invaluable as it provides the opportunity for children to manipulate the text and make changes without the often arduous process of rewriting.

Responding

> Children need to be trained in how to react to writing, particularly in how to think positively, focusing on what the writer has done best.
>
> (Parker, 1993)

Reacting to writing in a positive way does not necessarily come naturally to children. We need to acknowledge that this is a very sensitive area and, because of this, the role of the response partner should be discussed at some length with children. As experienced adult writers, we may often consult with a friend in order to achieve both reassurance and a more polished final product. It is important for both adults and children to know that any criticism of their writing should always be constructive and never destructive. A genuine response does not merely tell the writer what to do, instead, purposeful discussion allows children to make explicit what they implicitly know and adjust their writing accordingly. On some occasions, however, new knowledge may be passed on by the response partner, which writers can access for themselves in future work. By giving children opportunities to discuss their writing with a trusted peer or adult, we are giving them a real audience for their writing, an audience that can engage with the writer in crafting their text.

Oral and written feedback are both equally important. In some instances, however, it might be more helpful for writers to read their text aloud to their response partner. In this way, children will be listening for meaning, not reading for mistakes. They may wish to discuss their work at any stage during the writing process, not just at the end of a first or second draft. It can be very helpful for a child to receive feedback after the completion of a first paragraph where issues such as tone and voice (e.g. first or third person) are immediately evident. This allows the response partner to engage in the process of making meaning with the writer at an early point, and provides the opportunity for prediction as well as reflection. Figures 1.11 and 1.12 offer differentiated questions to support children's discussions and teachers may also want to modify the questions to make them specific to a particular genre.

The aim of the response partner should always be, first and foremost, to help the writer communicate within a text that has been constructed in a clear and purposeful way. By modelling the writing process, the teacher provides children with the opportunity to respond to her writing. At this point ground rules may be discussed and developed with the whole class so that sensitive approaches and clear procedures are established. Partnership is a key word in this relationship where, together, children will develop a growing confidence in responding to each other's writing and to receiving feedback from both peers and adults.

Response partners 1

Now, read your writing with your response partner.

Talk about these questions together.

Did you enjoy the writing?
Why?

Did you understand everything?

Is it a good beginning?
Why?

Is it a good ending?
Why?

Do you want to change anything?
If you do – what and why?

Figure 1.11   Response partners 1

© Pam Hodson and Deborah Jones (2001) *Teaching Children to Write*. London: David Fulton Publishers.

Response partners 2

Read your writing with your response partner.
Then discuss these questions together.

Did you enjoy the writing?
Why?

Did the beginning make you want to read more?
Why?

Was it a suitable ending?
Did it leave you satisfied or do you want to know more?

Think about the piece of writing as a whole.
Has anything been left out?
Are there any parts which you don't need?
Can you suggest different words – to make it clearer or more interesting?

Figure 1.12 Response partners 2

Presenting and publishing

> Publishing should be viewed as the end of a long process where the teacher works through the drafts with the child and both have agreed that the writing is good enough to be published.
>
> (Browne, 1996)

On some occasions, children will not want to publish their writing and we need to be sensitive to this fact; forcing publication may have a very negative effect. Personal writing such as diaries, journals or letters, often fulfil a very private purpose or are intended to be shared only between the teacher and the pupil. However, if they are particularly proud of a piece of work, there may be a natural desire to share this with a wider audience. One way of doing this, is by publishing in a specific format. Even at this stage, the process of decision making continues. For example, options of word processing or handwriting may be chosen. Children's work could become part of a larger display in which labels and captions are necessary or the writing itself could involve the inclusion of photographs and illustrations. A narrative or collection of poems may be published as a book to be shared with peers and adults and may eventually become part of the class or school library. Figure 1.13 is an invitation to select the most appropriate course of action and for many children, this stage of the process is the one they enjoy most.

Readers have choices and children need to be aware of this. In discussing publication with children, a range of teaching points may be made. A polished text in terms of accuracy, clarity of handwriting and general aesthetics is the reader's first point of contact. This initial encounter will result in the reader either exploring the text further, if their expectations are met, or discarding it. By sharing their writing with a wider audience, children become increasingly aware that more care needs to be taken with the finished product and this is an important part of their development as writers.

Presenting and publishing writing should be seen as a reflection of the value that both children and teachers attribute to their texts.

Reflecting

> A process approach often involves children reflecting on their own writing. This reflection could be on the written product, such as why certain decisions were made about what to include in the writing, or the actual process of writing. . . .
>
> (Graham and Kelly, 1998)

For all children, purposeful reflection should be an integral part of the whole writing process. Before children embark on a new piece of writing, it is essential to look back on what they have recently completed. This reflection can have many different purposes for children, to reflect on what they have learned, to identify key areas for development and to move them forward as writers.

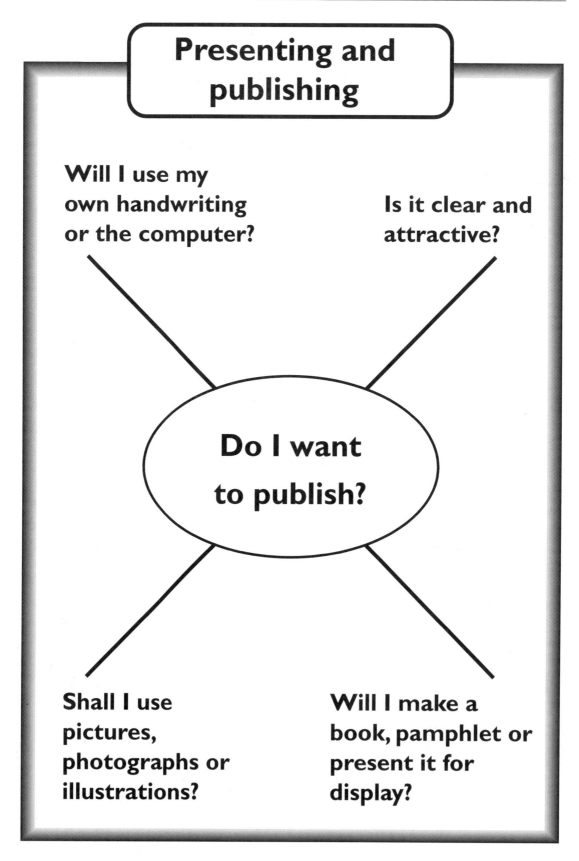

Figure 1.13   Presenting and publishing

© Pam Hodson and Deborah Jones (2001) *Teaching Children to Write*. London: David Fulton Publishers.

Reflection could take the form of a dialogue with the teacher, or it may be a private log for the child alone. It is the child, however, who should make that decision. Figure 1.14 offers children key questions to reflect on the whole writing process and to explore perceptions of themselves as writers. Although it is probably most common for children to reflect after publication, reflection can be employed at different stages of the writing process where it could involve a specific focus on features of the text such as vocabulary and sentence construction. By analysing their experiences of the writing process, children will be able to exercise more control over their own learning and gain the independence to move forward.

For children, reflection is essentially a vehicle for discovery: a discovery of themselves as real writers.

Target setting

> Targets spring from reviewing and reflecting upon work achieved . . . and are at the centre of the learning process. Setting targets consolidates and moves understanding forward, with the target conference providing an essential link between what has been learned and what the child still needs to know.
>
> (Jones, 2000)

An integral part of the reflection process concerns focusing on the writer's strengths and highlighting areas for development. Target setting should be part of an informed dialogue between the teacher and the child, in which they look closely at evidence produced at different stages of the writing process. This 'target conference' also provides the opportunity for children to discuss their 'Reflection' sheets with a trusted adult who enables them to elicit strategic goals and how they can be achieved. Figure 1.15 is a record to be kept by the children themselves, but in addition teachers, parents and peers may be given access to it. As method of recording and identifying future targets, it functions as a means of accountability and gives children greater control over their own learning. It also provides clear direction and makes the process of language development transparent within an atmosphere where learning is constructed jointly. Setting targets in this way, together with recording achievement, provides a powerful motivator for children.

Reflecting

If you want to record your responses in your journal or log, you can do so.

What was the writing about?

How did you start?

Where did you get your ideas from?

Did you reject any ideas? Why?

Were any parts difficult to write? Why?

Were any parts easy to write? Why?

Did you change your writing at all?
If so, what for?

Did you enjoy the writing?

How do you feel about the finished result?

Figure 1.14   Reflecting

© Pam Hodson and Deborah Jones (2001) *Teaching Children to Write*. London: David Fulton Publishers.

Target setting

Name:		

Targets	Date set:	Date achieved:

Figure 1.15   The process approach to writing: target setting

2 Writing narrative

This pattern (narrative) is common to almost all stories, from fairytale to adult novel. It probably explains why the form is so attractive to us for it allows us to develop extended communication with others and to structure the events of our lives in a way that has shape and significance.

(Parker, 1993)

Both the National Curriculum and the National Literacy Strategy emphasise the importance of narrative and story in children's writing development. All of us from an early age will have listened to stories and told stories and in that telling we will have captured moments, extended our experience into imagination and, at the same time, we will have shaped and consolidated new meanings. As adults, giving and receiving stories remains an integral part of our lives: narratives which may be encapsulated in speech or writing, in daily conversation or in reading a novel.

Most children will enter school with a great deal of implicit knowledge about how stories work and will generally show a willingness to write in story form. It is important, however, not to make too many assumptions about children's understanding of narrative structure. In order to develop their writing, we need to make story structure explicit to children and so build upon what they already know.

Many children at this early stage will realise that a story has a beginning, middle and end. Obviously this is very much an over-simplification and in order that children's knowledge of narrative structure should be extended, they need to be aware that the constituent elements of a story are more detailed.

One of the simpler models which analyses story structure has been recorded by the linguist Hoey (1983). This is how he perceives the basic pattern:

Situation	What was the situation?
Problem	What was the problem?
Solution	What was the solution?
Evaluation	How successful was it?

A more complex model was developed by Longacre (1976) who identifies the elements as follows:

Aperture	Opening, e.g. 'once upon a time'
Exposition	Essential information such as time, place, characters, etc.
Inciting moment	When things get going
Developing conflict	Intensification of action
Climax	Culmination of events
Denouement	Occurrence of a very important final event
Final suspense	Working out of details
Conclusion	Satisfactory result worked out

The writing frames which follow are designed to act as scaffolds for the child when planning a story and are based upon elements of models of narrative structure. They extend children's understanding of story and support the development of character and narrative voice. Obviously these writing frames need not be adhered to rigidly. Both teachers and pupils will modify them according to their needs but, underpinning the frameworks is the process model of writing, adapted specifically for the narrative genre.

The benefits of such an approach are many and imitate the process that real writers engage in whereby adult writers of fiction craft their work, taking it through successive drafts. Children, themselves, are empowered by the use of writing frames which enable them to realise that writing is not a process beyond their control. Eventually, the aim is that children will internalise the structures and gain independence as writers of fiction.

Narrative – making choices

The brainstorm

As we have already outlined in the previous chapter, children should be empowered to recognise that what they choose to write about is valid. This is as true of narrative as of any other genre. Above all, children should possess a clear sense of ownership of their own writing. One way of achieving this is by providing them with the opportunity to keep a record of ideas and topics which they might like to write about in the future. In this way, children maintain a real reason and purpose for writing.

Using the frame, 'Stories I want to write' (Figure 2.1) will provide children with a continuous stimulus. Besides being a self-generating fount of ideas, this also requires children to reflect on audience and purpose at the same time. From the outset then, they must consider notions of appropriacy in relation to their own ideas for writing. It may well be the case that not all the topics they have listed will be suited to the narrative form but the children's own ideas can be used as the basis for discussion about the appropriacy of different modes of writing.

The 'Story title' frame (Figure 2.2) in this section provides the opportunity for children to brainstorm ideas for one specific topic whereas Figure 2.3 is clearly focused and gives children greater direction. At the same time, however, it remains unsequenced, allowing children a more flexible approach to their stories.

Stories I want to write

WHAT do I want to write about?	WHY do I want to write it?	WHO do I want to write it for?

Figure 2.1 Narrative: Stories I want to write

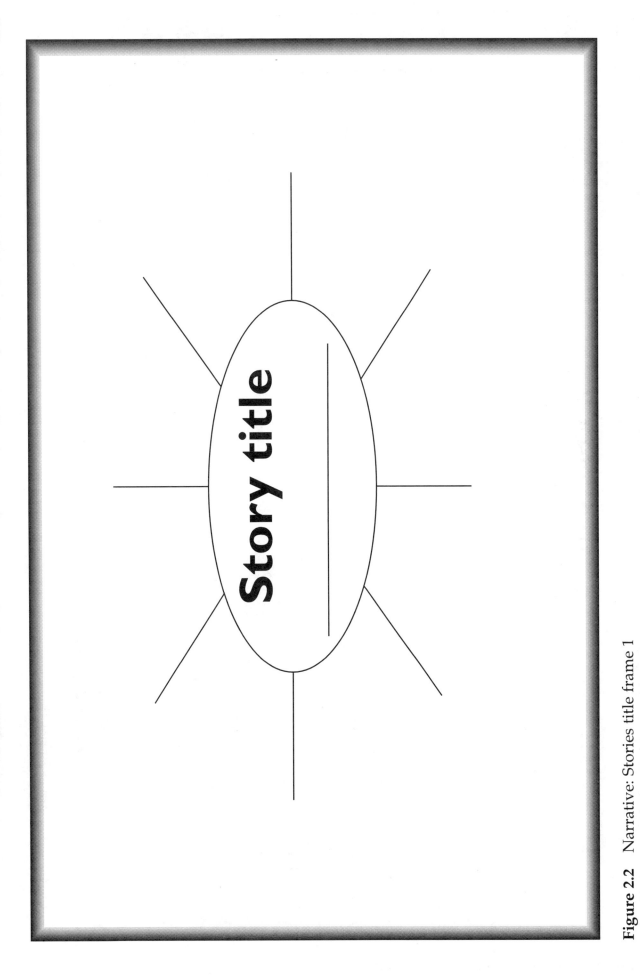

Figure 2.2   Narrative: Stories title frame 1

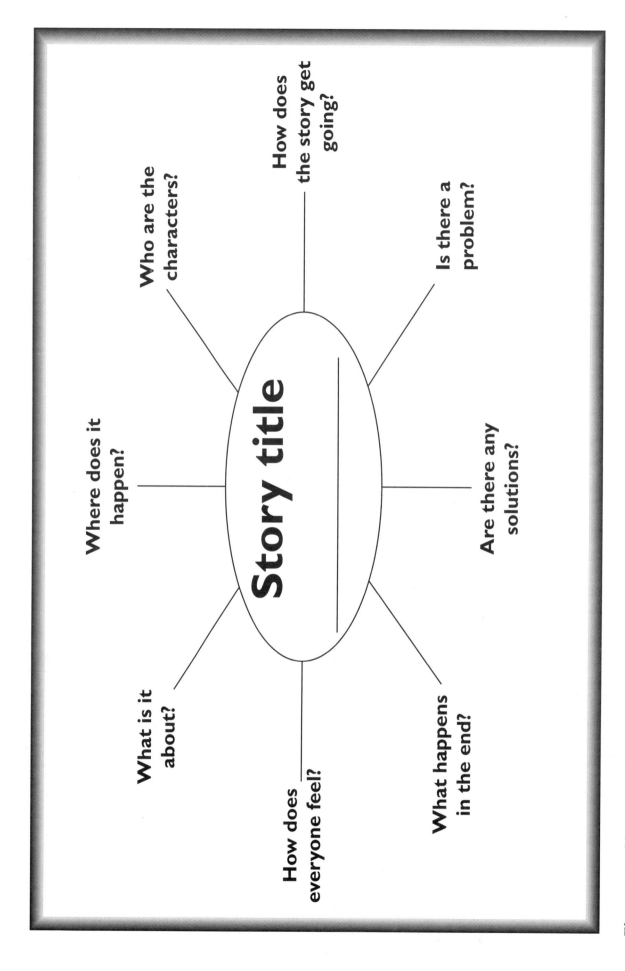

Figure 2.3 Narrative: Stories title 2

Sequencing and planning

Sequencing is a crucial part of any narrative writing. The following frames offer children the opportunity to plan different aspects of their stories and are differentiated so that teachers and pupils can select according to their particular needs and aims. Their use in practice has shown that children sometimes need directing as to which is the most appropriate frame for them, particularly in steering more able children to use the more complex model. The frames are not solely related to plot, although this obviously plays a major part in the planning of any chronological writing, but they also contain other elements integral to narrative, such as characters, narrative voice and setting.

The initial frame (Figure 2.4) has been left blank in order to allow children maximum flexibility. Therefore, they could choose to plan in picture form if this is the medium in which they feel most confident. This gives them the freedom to change the order of events by physically manipulating the boxes containing either words or pictures or, indeed, to match writing to their pictures at a later stage.

The more complex frames (Figures 2.5, 2.6 and 2.7) relate closely to the models of narrative outlined by Hoey and Longacre. They provide the children with the opportunity to reflect explicitly on the nature and structure of narrative. Not only do they enable them to think about these structures, but they provide different frameworks for shaping their thoughts and ideas.

The characters

The intention of the frames which focus on character is to increase children's awareness that characters should be developed and made multi-dimensional. A key element here is the widening and increasing sophistication of the children's vocabulary as they seek to create a character that is vivid, credible and integral to the plot (Figure 2.8). The appearance, actions and feelings of the character need to be considered from the outset so that the way children portray them is consistent throughout the narrative. (See Figures 2.9 and 2.10).

Enjoyment of the text often relies on the extent to which readers become involved with characters and so children need to be aware that they have the ability to evoke a response in the reader by the ways in which they choose to depict their characters. Implicit in all of this is the importance of considering audience. As children learn about this, they grow to understand that the characters they create can inspire sympathy and love and that this is a powerful tool for any writer.

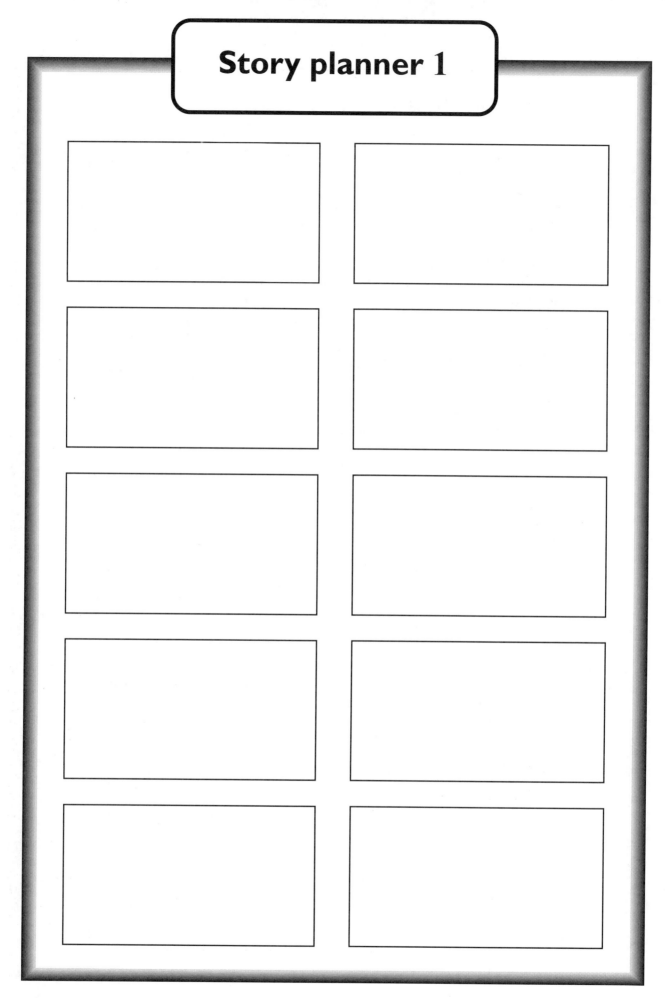

Figure 2.4 Narrative: Story planner 1

© Pam Hodson and Deborah Jones (2001) *Teaching Children to Write*. London: David Fulton Publishers.

Story planner 2

Who is in your story?

_____

_____

_____

_____

Where does it happen?

_____

_____

_____

_____

How does it start?

_____

_____

_____

_____

What happens in the end?

_____

_____

_____

_____

How does everyone feel?

_____

_____

_____

_____

Figure 2.5 Narrative: Story planner 2

Story planner 3

Starting off

What is it about?

Where does it happen?

Who are the characters?

Getting going

What happens?

Is there a problem?

Is it something exciting?

Sorting out

What happens next?

What do the characters do?

Are there possible solutions?

Finishing off

How does it end up?

How do the characters feel?

How do you feel?

Figure 2.6   Narrative: Story planner 3

Story Planner 4

Introduction

How is your story going to begin? Think about your first sentence.

Think about ...
where and when it happens, who the main characters are.

What happens to get the story going?

How does the action get more exciting?

Conclusion

Is there a satisfactory end to your story? Think about the last sentence.

How are all the final details worked out?

What happens to make the story work out?

What happens in the most exciting part of your story?

Figure 2.7 Narrative: Story Planner 4

© Pam Hodson and Deborah Jones (2001) *Teaching Children to Write*. London: David Fulton Publishers.

Zoom in- characters

What is your character's name?

What is s/he like?

When your story starts ...

What does s/he do?

How does s/he feel?

Why?

In the middle ...

What does s/he do?

How does s/he feel?

Why?

At the end ...

What does s/he do?

How does s/he feel?

Why?

Has anything changed this character?

If so – what and why?

Figure 2.8 Narrative: Zoom-in characters

© Pam Hodson and Deborah Jones (2001) *Teaching Children to Write*. London: David Fulton Publishers.

Characters in my story

Draw pictures of your characters.
Write their names underneath.

Write some words to show what they're like.

Write a bit about what they do.

At the end – how do they feel?

Figure 2.9 Narrative: Characters in my story

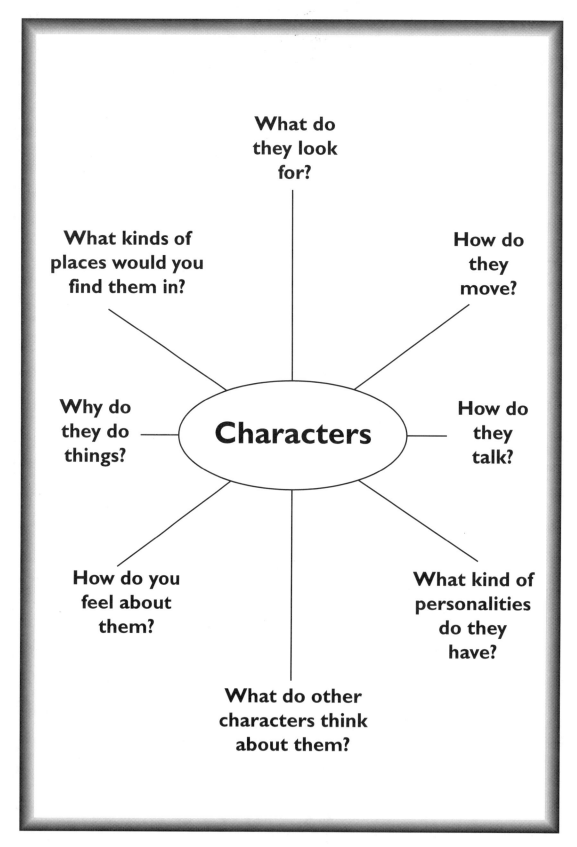

Figure 2.10 Narrative: Character development

© Pam Hodson and Deborah Jones (2001) *Teaching Children to Write*. London: David Fulton Publishers.

The narrator

A logical step following on from considerations about the characters in children's stories would be to identify who is actually telling the story, or how the story is to be told. To achieve a coherent and consistent narrative, children need to reflect explicitly on narrative voice and make decisions prior to writing which they will adhere to. Figure 2.11 draws children's attention to consider the key question of who tells their story or how their story is to be told. To achieve success in a narrative therefore, children need to reflect explicitly on narrative voice. If a narrator is the central character in the story, we need to help children understand what this really entails, such as writing in the first person whereas, an outside voice telling the story will be represented in the third person. Another point to be raised will focus on the use of tenses in relation to whether the storyteller is narrating events as they unfold, or from a position of knowledge after they have happened. Within such dialogue, children are encouraged to be consistent in their use of tenses and to be aware of the effects of changing tense within one particular narrative. This kind of reflection can promote relevant, and contextualised debate about grammar.

This leads children on to consider the area of narrative viewpoint and how much narrators know: do they have an all-knowing presence or do they in fact know less than both the characters within the story and the readers themselves (Figure 2.12).

Although these concepts may appear quite challenging, children will be implicitly aware of them from their own experiences of listening to and reading stories. Teachers need to build on this by providing models from the wealth of literature available which illustrates the variety and potential of narrative viewpoint. In this way the development of children's understanding and critical awareness of the conscious decisions made by story writers will feed back into their own writing and enrich the quality of their stories.

The setting

As with plot, character and narrative viewpoint, the depiction of setting is integral to a successful story and children will need opportunities to consider and plan where their story will be situated. A constructive way of promoting interesting and evocative description is to ask children to describe their setting in relation to the senses. Figure 2.13 provides structured questions which focus on sights, smells, sounds and textures. Again children can choose aspects of description which they consider to be relevant to their story rather than adopting a formulaic approach which includes all of these elements. Once children have made decisions, teachers could then focus on choosing appropriate adjectives and imagery, to portray the setting vividly.

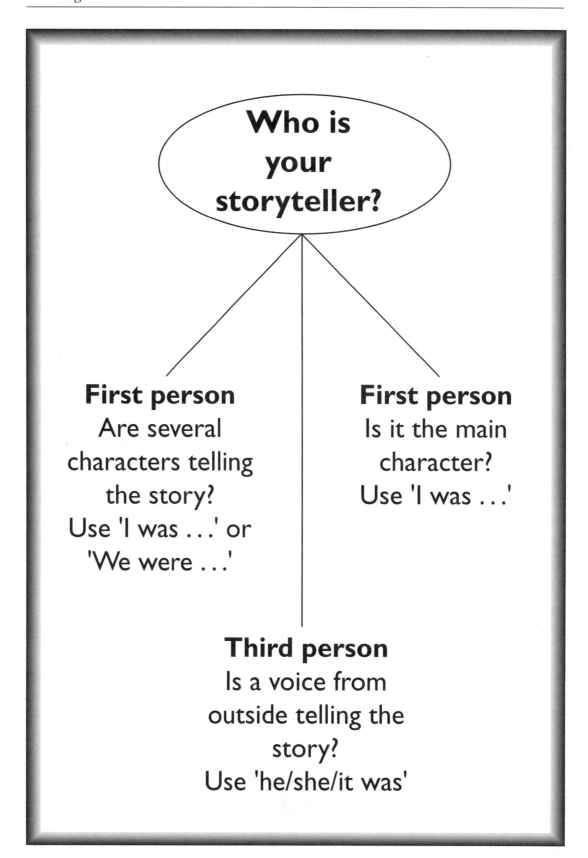

Figure 2.11   Narrative: Who is your storyteller?

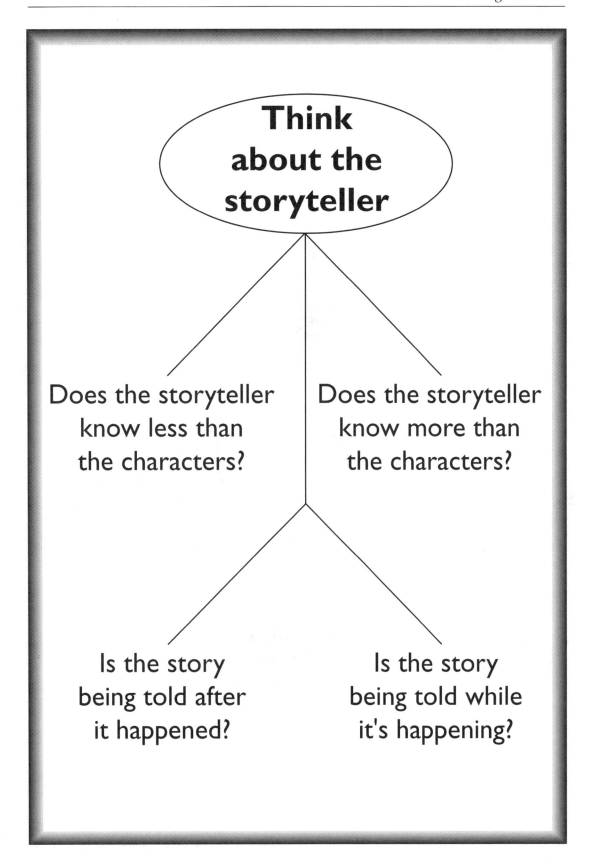

Figure 2.12 Narrative: Think about the storyteller

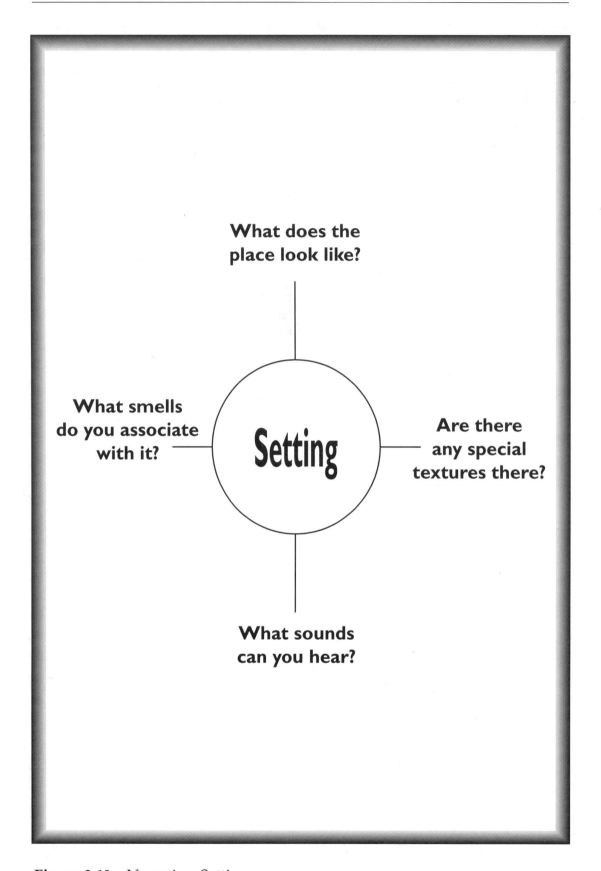

Figure 2.13 Narrative: Setting

© Pam Hodson and Deborah Jones (2001) *Teaching Children to Write*. London: David Fulton Publishers.

The aim of this chapter has been to identify discrete elements of the decision making process necessary for the construction of a successful narrative. When children are learning about story, teachers may wish to focus on one or two aspects of this process as a teaching tool, but at the same time remind children that all of these areas (structure, character, narrative voice and setting) combine to make an effective story. Once these decisions have been made, children can begin the drafting process and use the other strategies which have been outlined in Chapter 1.

3 Writing poetry

The most exciting sight of a new poem is often the messy early drafts, where we can see the poet thinking. The same is true of children. They need to understand that those early pieces of paper slashed with crossings-out . . . are the life blood of their learning and their poetry.

(Sedgwick, 1997)

Poetry offers enormous potential for teachers and pupils alike to explore language and, like any other form of writing, it is crafted. Children now have the opportunity to read poetry which reaches far beyond a narrow, traditional cannon. The language of advertising, jingles and slogans, can provide a focus for work and for many children, poetry is brought alive in schools by visits from 'real' poets. It is true that for some, teaching poetry can be problematic and often, the focus is on the end product, the neatly illustrated and presented piece to be displayed on the classroom wall. By adopting a process approach, however, useful strategies are provided for teachers while children have the opportunity to experiment with form and structure and to focus on language in an intensive way that is unique to poetry.

In order for children to be empowered as poets, they need to be exposed to a wide range of poetry, and not only material that is written for children. They should have a broad experience of poetry encompassing a range of forms, such as ballad, free verse, concrete poetry, etc. By extending the children's repertoire to include different forms of poetry, they will be provided with models that they can use during the course of their own writing. Writing poetry involves making decisions. In order to make these decisions, the children need to know the purpose of their writing and who they are writing it for. These factors, combined with the subject matter of the poem, will be very influential in deciding on form. Children who want to record particular events in their lives might choose the narrative or ballad form, whereas an exploration of personal feelings or ideas might lend itself more readily to free verse. As with any genre there are aspects which may inspire and some which may inhibit. For many children reared on a narrow diet of rhyming verse, poetry can become a straitjacket of words contrived to fit a regular rhyme scheme. On the other hand, a more positive aspect of writing poetry, is that the conciseness and structure that poetry offers can motivate even reluctant writers. Being aware of this and demonstrating sensitivity to children, whatever their starting points, is an important factor for teachers.

Another key issue for children is how to make the distinction between poetry and prose. It is the aim of this chapter to consider how to extend children's understanding of the ways in which they can craft poetry. In many ways poetry can be a great liberator, because it allows children to give shape to their ideas and allows them to experiment with language in its widest sense. It is the teacher's role, therefore, to extend their horizons and make children aware of the enormous potential that poetry has to offer.

Making decisions

As with all forms of writing, children should be encouraged to display autonomy in the decision-making process. The first decision will probably focus around the topic for the poem. Therefore, the children should be encouraged to explore a range of topics which may stem from personal experience or from something they have watched or read. The chosen topic has to be considered in relation to why they are writing it and who they are writing it for (see Figure 3.1). Teachers need to be very sensitive to these issues as some poetry written by children is of an essentially personal nature and is not intended for a public audience.

The brainstorm

The brainstorm can liberate children and free them from restrictions of form, rhyme or rhythm to explore all of the issues that they might cover in relation to their topic. (See Figure 3.2). This might lead them to re-focus their ideas and realise that just one aspect of their chosen topic could furnish them with enough material to develop into a poem.

Describing ideas

At this stage of the composing process, it is important for children to realise that poetry is carefully crafted and that poets may take days to deliberate over the choice of particular words or phrases. Figure 3.3 allows them to identify specific features of their chosen topic and to consider how best they might be described. It is helpful here to steer children away from using clichés and use this time to extend children's vocabulary. Exploring appropriate and powerful adjectives to describe people, places or objects, provides a rich opportunity for developing, in context, knowledge of grammatical terms.

Shaping

At this stage, children should still not feel that they have to conform to any pre-identified form of poetry. Figure 3.4 enables them to explore the potential of poetry by playing with the length and arrangement of lines. This is a very important area to address as often, children can produce pieces of writing which sound like poetry, but do not look like poetry on the page. It is

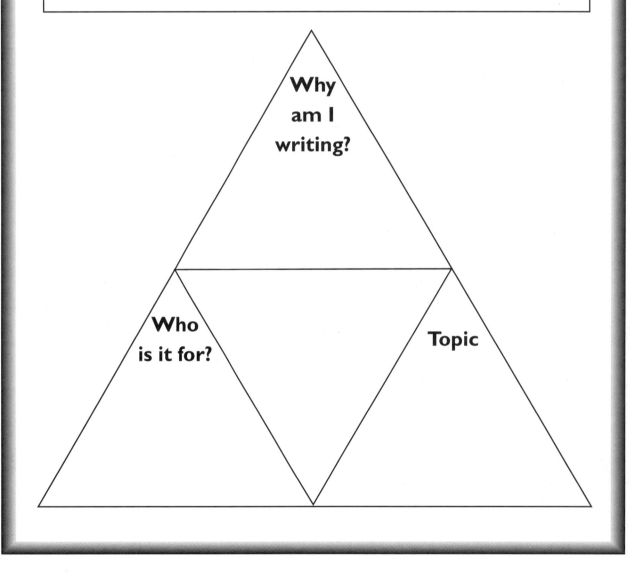

Making decisions

Think of some topics, ideas and issues
you would like to write about.
Put them down here.

Choose the one you would like to write
about first _____

Why
am I
writing?

Who
is it for?

Topic

Figure 3.1 Poetry: Making decisions

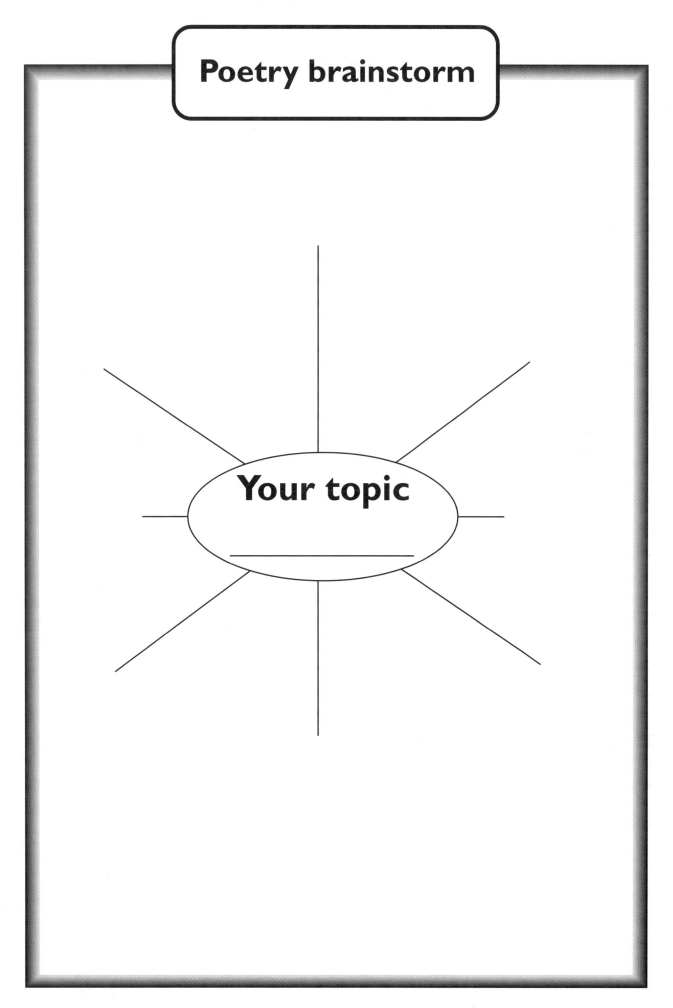

Figure 3.2   Poetry brainstorm

Idea	Description	Idea	Description	Idea	Description

Describing ideas

Figure 3.3 Poetry: Describing ideas

Poetry-shaping

List your ideas for your poem below.
Remember, each line does not have to be
a sentence – it might be just one or two words.

_____

_____

_____

_____

_____

_____

_____

_____

_____

Re-read your poem.
Do you want to change the order of the lines?
Does your poem have a rhyme scheme?
Do you want it divided into verses?

Figure 3.4 Poetry-shaping

important for the teacher to highlight the flexibility of poetry by modelling this process for them or writing with them collaboratively. This provides both teacher and children with the opportunity to reflect on how powerful the positioning of a word on the line can be, the effect of choosing a particular line-break and the appropriacy of rhyme.

Matching

Implicit in this part of the creative process is the understanding that children have been exposed to the forms of poetry that are identified in Figure 3.5 and have explored their potential. An explicit consideration of the sonnet, for example, will lead children to make informed decisions on whether it is an appropriate form for them to use in their own poetry. In this way, children are using and applying their own knowledge in the matching of their ideas to an appropriate form. Figure 3.5 acts as a prompt for children to consider which form they will adopt and obviously can be adapted by the teacher to reflect the experience of the children.

First draft

Before reaching this point, children will have gone through several essential stages. By engaging in these processes, they will have had the opportunity to explore many relevant and exciting aspects of language. When writing their first draft, (Figure 3.6), children need to be reassured that this first draft is malleable and can be altered. One way of doing this is to suggest using a response partner who can provide a receptive ear to helping the writer improve their poem. A second or third draft may follow, but these need not necessarily be written on separate sheets of paper. Within this process of drafting, children should also be encouraged to put a line through words, rather than rub them out, as ultimately, they may find they will choose a word or phrase which appeared in an initial draft. In many ways, seeing evidence of texts changing can give children a sense of progress and development.

Revising and proof-reading

Sedgwick quotes the words of the French writer, Paul Valery, who says that, 'a poem is never finished, only abandoned'. However, there will come a time when children wish to bring their poem towards a conclusion. At this point, it is appropriate for them to reflect on the final draft and consider crucial issues such as the shape of the poem on the page and the length of verses and lines. When the child is happy that the poem communicates the desired message, transcriptional issues such as spelling and punctuation can be addressed. Figure 3.7 provides questions and prompts that enable them to do this.

Matching

**Think about what form of poetry
will suit your writing best.**

Will it be . . .

Haiku

Acrostic

Ballad

Sonnet

Limerick

Concrete verse

Free verse

Ode

Other . . .

Figure 3.5   Poetry: Matching

© Pam Hodson and Deborah Jones (2001) *Teaching Children to Write*. London: David Fulton Publishers.

Poetry – first draft

Title: _____

Read your poem aloud to a friend.
Does it sound right?
Do you want to add any words?
Do you want to change any words?
Do you want to cross out any words?
Re-read your poem aloud
after you've made any changes.

Figure 3.6   Poetry – First draft

Revising and proof-reading poetry

Re-read your poem. You might like to consider these questions on your own or with a partner:

• Does the poem say what you want it to say?

• Are you happy with the shape of your poem?

• Where have you put capital letters and full stops? *Remember in poetry, each new line can begin with a capital letter; the end of a line does not mean it is the end of a sentence. Full stops can come in the middle of a line. You can decide.*

Use this code:

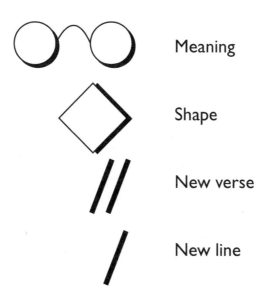

Meaning

Shape

New verse

New line

Figure 3.7   Revising and proof-reading poetry

© Pam Hodson and Deborah Jones (2001) *Teaching Children to Write.* London: David Fulton Publishers.

Presenting

It is a familiar sight to see children's poems displayed on walls and in class anthologies either word-processed or handwritten, but poems can be presented in a range of imaginative and creative ways other than just written on the paper. This creativity can be extended further, as children consider whether they wish to record their poem on tape perhaps using music, to engage other friends in a group reading or to extend the images into a visual representation or painting. Figure 3.8 provides them with a variety of options from which they may select, linking the presentation of poetry with other art forms which can be a highly creative and stimulating process which gives depth and richness to children's experiences.

Reflecting

Once children have engaged in composing their poems, it is important to provide them with the opportunity to think about the process. Figure 3.9 encourages them to reflect explicitly on the decisions and difficulties they have encountered and how they feel about the finished product. In this way, children will develop their understanding of the rich and complex nature of poetry and be able to use their new knowledge in future work.

Presenting

Will I present my poem as . . .

Mime

Music

Video

Cassette recording

A shape

A drawing

A painting

Movement

Several of these?

Figure 3.8 Presenting poetry

© Pam Hodson and Deborah Jones (2001) *Teaching Children to Write*. London: David Fulton Publishers.

Reflecting

Why did you write
your poem?

Did you change
your poem?
Why?

How do
you feel
about the
finished
result?

Did you reject
any ideas?
Why?

Where did
your ideas
come from?

How did you
feel when you
were writing?

Was starting writing
difficult or easy?
Why?

Figure 3.9   Reflecting on poetry

4 | Writing non-fiction

In learning to write, children are involved in learning to recognise and learn the different ways in which meanings are shaped in written texts. That is, they are learning to control the different genres.

(Czerniewska, 1992)

The current English National Curriculum and the National Literacy Strategy have highlighted the importance of providing children with the opportunities to write both fiction and non-fiction texts. In the previous two chapters we have focused on fiction by exploring how narrative and poetry are constructed but within the non-fiction category there are also different genres (here, the term genre is used to indicate the form and structure of the text). By analysing these different structures, a variety of different text types can be identified. For the purposes of this chapter, we will be using the categories adopted by the National Literacy Strategy in *The National Literacy Strategy: Grammar for Writing 2000*. (See Figure 4.1 below).

Text types

- Recount
- Non-chronological report
- Instructions and procedures
- Explanation
- Persuasion
- Discussion

Figure 4.1   Non-fiction – text types

The explicit teaching of non-fiction has a comparatively short history within England and Wales and presents challenges to both teachers and pupils. However, to be effective writers, children need to become proficient in using a variety of forms. We have already explored the complexities of writing an extended narrative, but in the world beyond the classroom, adults are more likely to be engaged in writing for functional reasons, whether noting down a shopping list or crafting a formal letter. As a result of listening to and reading stories, children become familiar with the narrative form from an early age and it is this they will initially use and resort to for writing, particularly if they lack the knowledge and experience of how particular texts are constructed. A further issue that may arise in non-fiction writing, is that its vocabulary and grammar is further removed from the language and patterns of everyday speech than narrative. The use of writing frames is particularly useful in providing the necessary scaffold to support children as they begin to address these points.

Writing non-fiction, however, does provide children with real purposes and audiences and this can prove to be a very positive motivational factor. An obvious example of this is when children write a letter collaboratively to invite a poet to visit the school. When children receive a positive response, they begin to realise the power of the appropriate written form to achieve a desired outcome. As they become more secure in this knowledge, and develop their confidence in using different forms, children are empowered to function as successful members of society.

Within school, non-fiction texts are used across the whole curriculum and children are expected to write in a way that is matched to different subjects, such as recording a maths investigation or writing a report of a visit. The National Literacy Strategy has highlighted the need to teach the skills required explicitly to operate across a wide range of non-fiction genres. Once children have learned how to construct writing in this genre, they can transfer these skills into a range of subjects.

Because many children find the structures and words within non-fiction unfamiliar, the teacher plays a key role in providing children with models of different texts. Before writing begins, the teacher will need to read examples of a specific text type with children, drawing their attention to the particular structure and features of that form. Teachers may find it helpful to annotate an enlarged text, indicating the specific elements of the genre; these can be left on the wall as a point of reference. Clearly, the more children become familiar with reading these forms, the more confident they will become in their own writing.

An important part of composing any non-fiction text is to gather and select appropriate facts and information. Teachers need to show children different strategies for taking notes otherwise there is a danger that children may simply copy from an original source. The teacher can model techniques such as superimposing acetates over big books or enlarged texts and then underlining key words and phrases in whole class sessions; children can then duplicate this process in smaller groups. In this way children's attention is drawn to specific aspects or themes giving them a clear focus for the particular information they need to extract in order to form the basis for their own writing. For some forms of writing, note taking is unnecessary as the information may be stored in the child's head and can be noted by using a simple brainstorm.

Once the relevant information has been selected, by modelling discrete text types in both shared and guided writing sessions, the teacher will then move on to giving children first hand experience of writing texts for a specific purpose and audience. At this stage, teachers can discuss particular features of the text type with children making them aware of the explicit choices of grammar, sentence construction and vocabulary they will need to make.

Encouraging independence in children underpins the whole of the process approach to writing and one way of developing this is to provide models of different text types which they can access easily. As well as having examples displayed around the classroom, resource boxes containing different examples of writing such as advertisements, newspaper reports, recipes, etc. can be made available. In addition, children could include their own writing and bring examples from home to add to the resource boxes as and when they wish.

Within non-fiction, there exists a wide variety of different forms and the boundaries between different text types are not always clearly defined. As a result, teachers will probably choose to adapt the generic frames included in this section according to the specific requirements and different contexts of the writing.

Collaboration should be an integral part of the writing process and one way of fostering this is by using the 'Notes' space that is included in many of the frames. This can be used by the teacher to indicate key features of grammar, vocabulary or to record questions for the child to consider which will move their writing forward. Once an initial draft has been completed, it is helpful for children to be given time for sharing their drafts with peers or response partners who may also use the box as a means of communicating suggestions for improvement. Equally, the more independent writer may use the boxes as a way of recording ideas as and when they emerge; these can be inserted into the text later.

The rest of this chapter explores the six text types that we have identified within non-fiction. For each one, there is a selection of writing frames or prompts which, when used in conjunction with the process approach, offers a coherent system for teaching non-fiction writing.

Recount

Children are probably most familiar with recount as it may easily be linked to their personal experience and topics of interest. The purpose of the recount is to retell events and incidents, in a way which could inform or entertain the audience.

Within the recount genre there are a variety of different types of writing which children will come to recognise such as biographies, autobiographies, diaries and newspaper reports. However, it would be true to say that a newspaper report for example, could also be categorised as persuasive writing and this highlights the difficulty in defining boundaries for writing. Rather than perceiving these issues as problems, they can be used to develop children's understanding of the subtleties of language and the complex way in which it works.

Using the frames

The brainstorm (Figure 4.2) allows children to record their initial thoughts and ideas in response to key questions which focus on what actually happened, where the events took place, who was involved and why it happened. As this particular type of writing is chronological, one of the most important skills involved is that of sequencing. In Figure 4.3 children are asked to refer back to the 'what' question in their brainstorm and put in order the details they have noted. The sequencing frame offers additional support by suggesting key connectives that can then be incorporated into a first draft. Of course some children may be more comfortable about using pictures rather than words and this use of pictures should be regarded as an intermediate stage which allows children to build their confidence and record ideas quickly. As a next step, they should be encouraged to construct texts, using the pictures to support their writing.

Figures 4.4 and 4.5 offer two differentiated frames to support children in writing their first draft. Their purpose is to make the structure of the recount genre explicit both in its organisation and sentence structure. When using these, children are required to draw on the work recorded in the brainstorming and sequencing sheets and fit what they have already done into the structures offered by the first draft frames. Connectives, specific to chronological writing will be a key teaching point and the Notes column draws attention to these. Figure 4.4 provides children with key questions to help them remember the structure, followed by starter sentences to initiate the writing. A more sophisticated frame is offered in Figure 4.5 which identifies different aspects of the recount genre by using metalanguage such as 'orientation', 'events' and 're-orientation'. In order to support children's independent writing, the frame also offers key questions and appropriate connectives.

Non-chronological reports

The term 'report' is used loosely within society and children will be familiar with the terms 'news report', 'football report' or 'weather report'. For the purposes of this chapter, we use the term 'report' to describe or present factual information about both living and non-living things. A major challenge for children in writing these texts is that they are not structured chronologically, so providing them with writing frames offers support in understanding this particular genre. Although the frames make the distinction between living and non-living things, the nature of report writing means that the exact sentence starters or questions will differ significantly according to the subject matter which will in turn, drive the particular vocabulary. Because of this it is particularly difficult to provide generic frames and teachers will adapt the frames according to the specific focus of the writing.

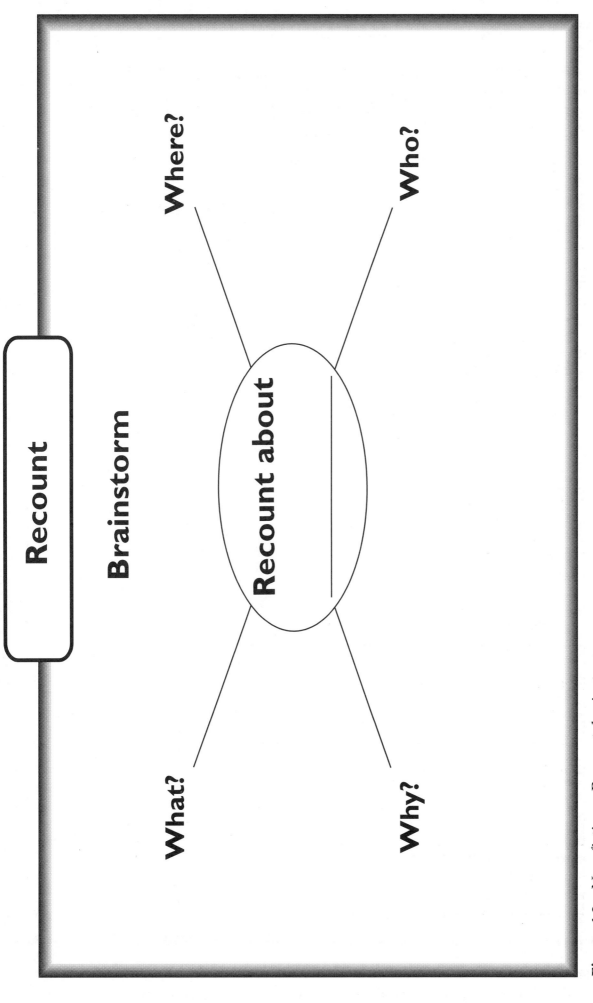

Figure 4.2 Non-fiction – Recount: brainstorm

Recount

Sequencing

What happened? Use your response to the brainstorm. Try and record in the order events happened. You can use pictures or words or both.

First

Then

Later

After

Finally

Notes

Figure 4.3 Non-fiction – Recount: sequencing

Recount

First draft (a)

My recount is about _____

_____

Where did it happen? Who was there?	**Notes:**
_____ took place in	Connectives to use: until, meanwhile, after
_____	
_____ and _____ were there.	

What happened? (use your flow diagram to get the right order).

First

Then

Next

Later

How do you want to sum up?

The last thing to say is _____

_____

Figure 4.4   Non-fiction – Recount: first draft (a)

Recount

First draft (b)

Title: _____

Orientation:

Who was there?

Where was it?

Why were they there?

Events:

What happened? •

Why? •

  •

  •

  •

  •

Re-orientation:
How would you sum up the event?

Notes:
Key connectives: because, although, so, therefore, consequently, later, subsequently, before, in the beginning

Figure 4.5   Non-fiction – Recount: first draft (b)

Using the frames

Before children begin to structure their information, they will need to brainstorm their ideas, perhaps on a blank sheet of paper where they can note down everything they know, or have read, about this particular subject. Figure 4.6 is particularly appropriate for a young child or one who experiences difficulties in writing and presents a basic structure for organising a report which can incorporate both pictures and words. The main purpose of these frames is to help children organise their ideas and in completing them, they should still be using note form. This is developed in Figures 4.7 to 4.10 which offer sentence starters that provide a prompt for children to write their first draft.

Instructional or procedural texts

These types of texts show or describe how something can be done by following a series of steps and could take the form of recipes, rules for playing games, instructions for making a model, and so on. Children can be highly motivated to read and write within this genre as the outcome can be both practical and immediate. Because of this, it is easy to find real reasons for writing which will be an integral part of classroom practice. For example, after children have finished a science investigation, they can be asked to give written instructions to another group on how to carry out the activity. They can readily assess how effective their writing has been by the group's ability to complete the task.

Using the frames

Figure 4.11 is a simple frame that requires children to identify the focus for their instructions, the items needed in order to carry out these instructions and the logical sequence they should follow. Children should be made aware that although the format encourages them to write in the correct order, at this stage the writing is still malleable and arrows could be used to reorganise instructions if necessary. Again, pictures can be used in conjunction with words as an aid to recording relevant details.

In writing instructional texts, children also need to consider whether it is appropriate to incorporate pictures or diagrams as an additional aid to understanding. This is where examining a variety of models can inform children's decisions and help them see how different types of visual images (photographs, diagrams, illustrations) can support both the reading and writing of this particular genre.

As discussed earlier, the instructional genre offers a range of organisational features and Figures 4.12 and 4.13 make the range of possibilities explicit. Children need to decide whether to use numbers, bullet points or separate sentences to indicate the sequence of their instructions. Whatever the decision, it is important for children to understand that each point should concern only a single action. They could, in fact, experiment with all of them and then choose the structure they feel is the most appropriate.

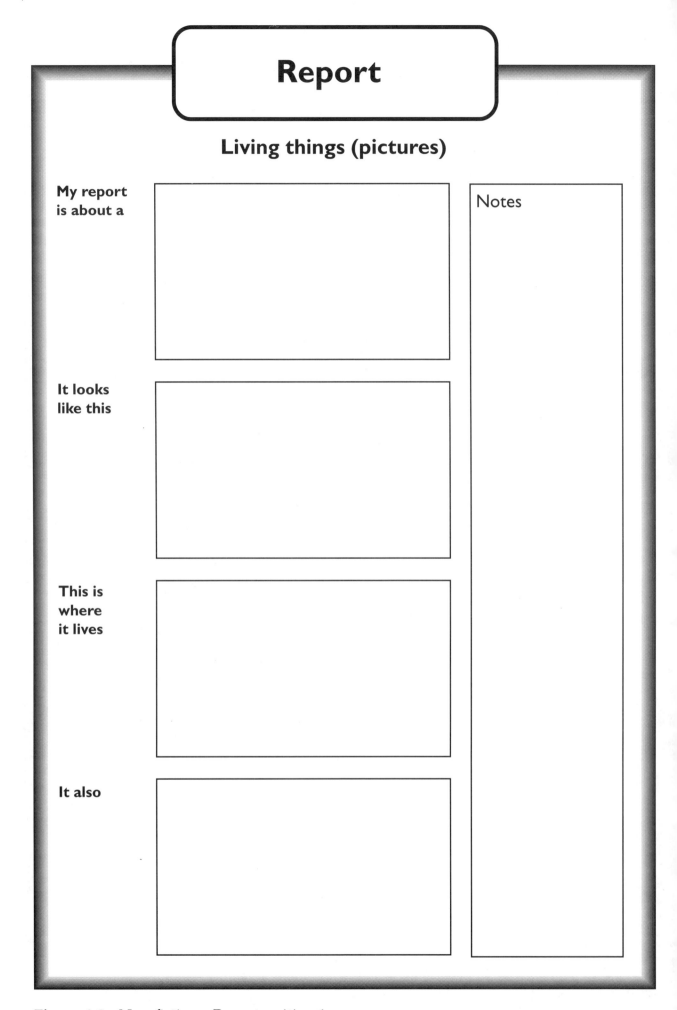

Figure 4.6 Non-fiction – Report writing 1

Report

Living things

What is your report about?	Notes

What kind of thing is it? Does it belong to a particular family?

What does it look like?

Where does it live?

What does it live on/eat?

What else do you know about it?

Figure 4.7 Non-fiction – Report writing 2

Report

Non-living things

What is your report about?	Notes
What kind of object is it? Does it belong to a particular group?	
What does it look like?	
What does it do?	
How does it work?	
What else do you know about it?	

Figure 4.8 Non-fiction – Report writing 3

© Pam Hodson and Deborah Jones (2001) *Teaching Children to Write*. London: David Fulton Publishers.

Report

Living things

The _____ is a _____
_____

It is part of the _____ family.

The _____ has _____
_____ and _____

It can be found _____
_____

The _____ eats _____
_____

Other interesting things about _____
_____ are that _____
_____

Notes

Figure 4.9 Non-fiction – Report writing 4
© Pam Hodson and Deborah Jones (2001) *Teaching Children to Write*. London: David Fulton Publishers.

Report

Non-living things

	Notes
The _____ is a _____ _____	
It is part of the _____ family.	
The _____ has _____ _____ and _____	
It can be found _____ _____	
The _____ eats _____ _____	
Other interesting things about _____ _____ are that _____ _____	

Figure 4.10 Non-fiction – Report writing 5

© Pam Hodson and Deborah Jones (2001) *Teaching Children to Write*. London: David Fulton Publishers.

Instructions

How to	Notes
Things you need	
What you need to do	

Pictures	Words

⬇ ⬇

⬇ ⬇

⬇ ⬇

Figure 4.11 Non-fiction – Instructions 1

© Pam Hodson and Deborah Jones (2001) *Teaching Children to Write*. London: David Fulton Publishers.

Instructions

Goal	Notes
What needs to be achieved:	
Materials/equipment needed:	

Words	Diagrams

Figure 4.12 Non-fiction – Instructions 2

© Pam Hodson and Deborah Jones (2001) *Teaching Children to Write*. London: David Fulton Publishers.

Instructions

How to:

In order to make a _____ you will need:

1.

2.

3.

4.

First you

Next

Then

Finally

Notes

· · · ·

Ask a friend to try out this explanation. Can they do it? Write the comments in the Notes box.

Figure 4.13   Non-fiction – Instructions 3

Another key teaching point is to highlight the sentence structure used in writing this type of text. Verbs, indicating commands often appear at the beginning of a sentence, for example, a recipe may begin, 'Take two large eggs. . . .' Whereas in many forms of writing, teachers would encourage children to write their sentences in different ways, within this particular genre, it is perfectly valid to repeat sentence constructions.

Once this frame has been completed, a response partner can evaluate the effectiveness of the writing. The writer is successful if the reader is confident that they can complete the instructions and if they are unable to do so, the response partner can indicate where the writing lacks clarity. In this way, children can be helped to re-draft their texts.

Explanation

This is a genre that children are familiar with as they will have encountered it in science, history and geography texts. In the world outside the classroom, the doctor's surgery for example, they will probably have seen and read many pamphlets or leaflets which set out to explain how to do things or what something is.

As with all genres, it is very important for children to consider who they are writing for and it can be helpful in promoting clarity and precision of writing for them to think about the reader as a non-specialist in the chosen subject. This time spent discussing the chosen audience with its particular needs, will help children to craft their explanations in a more focused way.

Using the frames

In producing an explanation it is useful for children to think about the key questions their readers will need answers to in order to help them understand the chosen topic. Figure 4.14 is a brainstorm which asks a range of generic questions such as 'How does it happen?' or 'What is it used for?' It is important to stress to children that in some instances not all these questions will be relevant to their particular explanation. On the other hand, the question 'What else do you know?' encourages them to note any additional information which they have not already included.

In writing an explanation, children may wish to use a lot of technical vocabulary. A glossary may be used as a strategy to maintain conciseness in the children's writing, and at the same time, to ensure that the reader understands the explanation. Figure 4.15 presents a structure for writing a glossary and highlights the importance of using technical language within explanations. Again, showing children models of glossaries in various formats will expand their knowledge and understanding of this device, while creating their own will enable children to produce clearer and more focused explanations. Producing a glossary also entails the writing of definitions which in itself is an important skill children need to learn.

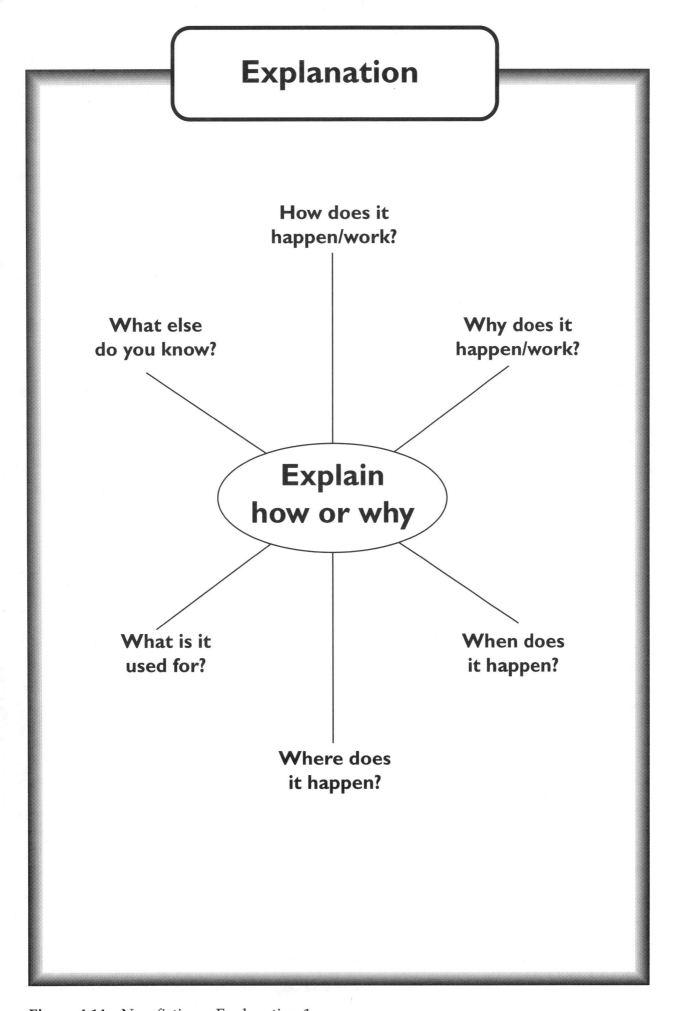

Figure 4.14 Non-fiction – Explanation 1

Explanation

Glossary

Key word:

[ ]

Explanation:

[ ]

Key word:

[ ]

Explanation:

[ ]

Key word:

[ ]

Explanation:

[ ]

Figure 4.15   Non-fiction – Explanation 2

© Pam Hodson and Deborah Jones (2001) *Teaching Children to Write*. London: David Fulton Publishers.

The first draft frame (Figure 4.16) provides a structure for explanations using sentence starters, while Figure 4.17 provides a more advanced version requiring the child to write under subheadings. The main body of the second frame reflects and orders the questions asked within the brainstorm so children will find it useful to refer directly to this when composing their first draft. Both frames ask children to consider how diagrams or photographs would enhance their explanations and both draw attention to the use of relevant connectives within the 'Notes' column. As with procedural texts, explanatory texts particularly lend themselves to being shared with a response partner. Space is given for comments to be written either by this critical friend, or by the writer after hearing the response, which may in turn lead on to clarification of the text within a second draft.

Persuasion

In today's society, children will be bombarded by literature of all kinds that attempts to convince them to do or to buy certain things. Advertisements are a prime illustration of persuasive material; these can take an overtly persuasive form or can be extremely subtle. Estate agents and travel agents may appear to give information, but actually seek to persuade the reader to buy. This genre can be very manipulative, so it is important that children, from an early age, learn to read it critically. In writing this genre, children need to know about the importance of tone and voice and, of course, linked closely with this, are considerations of audience and purpose. When preparing a piece of persuasive writing, children should be shown the importance of selecting facts and information which are relevant to their purpose so that they can persuade the reader. In this section, the focus is on a specific type of persuasive writing where children are taught to argue the case for a particular point of view.

Using the frames

Figure 4.18 provides a structure for presenting a simple argument. The child is required to make an initial statement which outlines their point of view. They then develop this with as many reasons as they can; the final sentence or paragraph reiterating and reaffirming the opening statement.

The following two frames, (4.19 and 4.20) are designed to show some of the specific devices which can be used in persuasion. The starter sentences in Figure 4.19 adopt the first person and employ a friendly informal tone which attempts to engage the reader, but children also need to be able to adopt a more impersonal tone and use the third person. This is shown in Figure 4.20 where the structure remains basically the same but children are encouraged to develop and elaborate their point of view by including evidence. It also addresses the issue that in a more sophisticated persuasion, children may also wish to consider an opposing argument which they then counter.

Explanation

Title: How or why
I am going to explain why/how

The reasons for this are that	Notes Connectives: then, next, later, because, so
and	
also	
Another reason may be that	

So all these things show why

Do you want to use drawings or photographs for your work? Ask a friend to read this. Do they understand everything?

Figure 4.16 Non-fiction – Explanation 3

Explanation

Title: How or why . . . .

General statement to introduce the subject:

Give an explanation:

- how it happens/works

- why it happens/works

- when it happens/works

- where it happens/works

- what the point is/what it's used for

Summarise the main points:

Check: Do I want to use photographs/diagrams/ pictures to make my explanation clearer?
Give it to someone else to read.

Notes

Figure 4.17 Non-fiction – Explanation 4

Persuasion

I think that

I think this because

-
-
-
-
-

Notes

Summing up, I have shown that

so

Figure 4.18   Non-fiction – Persuasion 1

© Pam Hodson and Deborah Jones (2001) *Teaching Children to Write*. London: David Fulton Publishers.

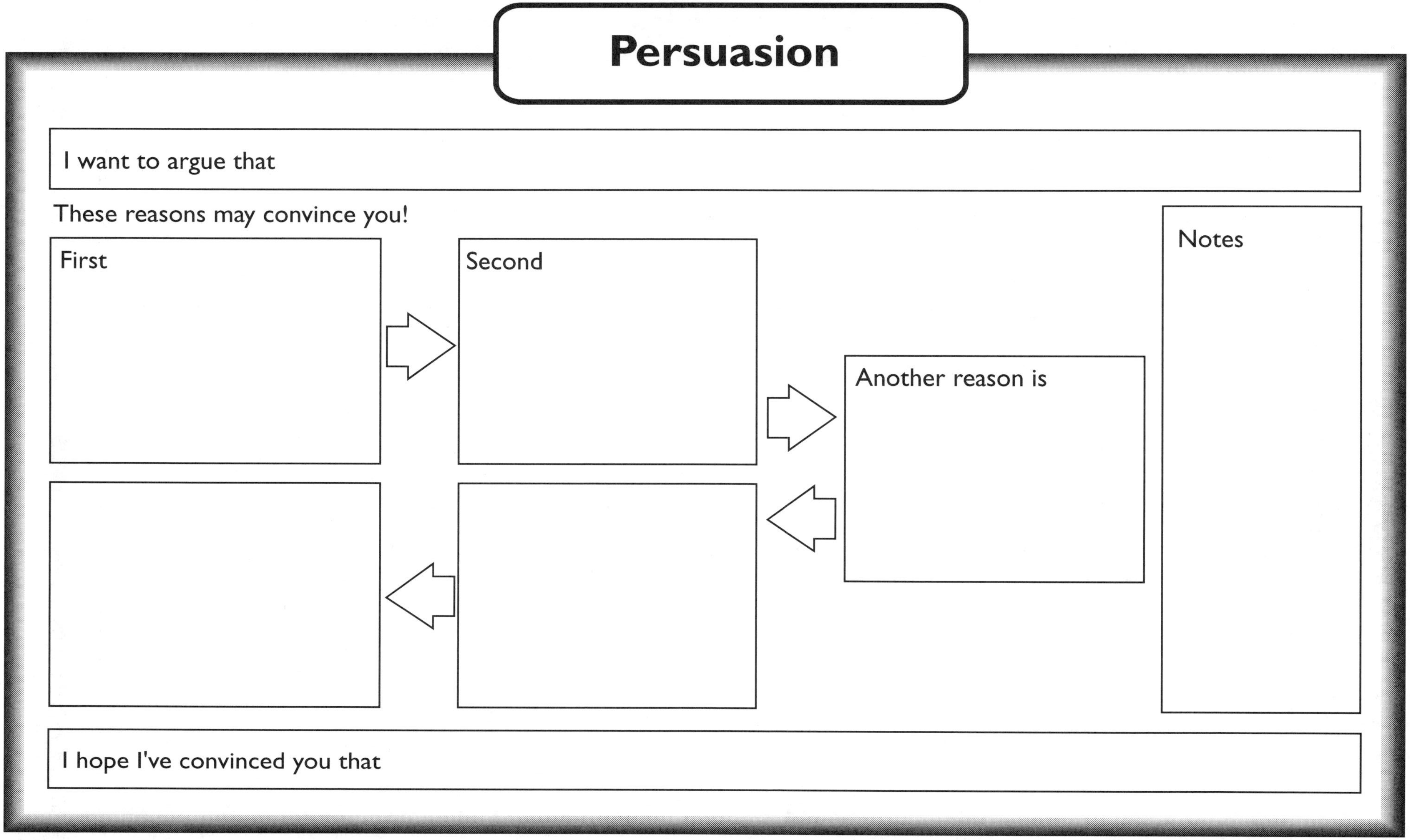

Persuasion

I want to argue that

These reasons may convince you!

First

Second

Another reason is

I hope I've convinced you that

Notes

Figure 4.19 Non-fiction – Persuasion 2

© Pam Hodson and Deborah Jones (2001) *Teaching Children to Write*. London: David Fulton Publishers.

Persuasion

Opening statement of point of view:

Key points/facts	Elaboration and development of points with evidence	Notes
•		
•		
•		
•		
• It is sometimes said that	However	

Summary or re-statement of opening point:

Figure 4.20 Non-fiction – Persuasion 3

Discussion

This can be seen as a natural progression from persuasive writing. In developing a discussion, children will be expected to present arguments reflecting different points of view which are supported by evidence. This genre can pose many challenges to young children. An effective discussion will involve not only good ideas, but a clear and logical structure which is in turn, backed up by evidence and reaches a considered conclusion. In order to fuel their debates, children will get their information from a variety of sources, whether written texts, media or their own knowledge and experience.

When asking children to prepare a discussion, reading for information can provide the basis for ideas and facts but the processes involved in planning and shaping a spoken, formal debate, either in whole class or group situations, can mirror the organisation necessary for written discussion. Children can be asked to present their points of view to the class, working from their written notes. Equally, children may discuss an issue together and then reflect, organise and formulate their written discussion. It is clear then that reading, writing, speaking and listening all have an important role to play.

Using the frames

Within this more complex genre, children could be overwhelmed by the volume of material with which they are initially faced. Because of this, the purpose for their research needs to be made clear from the beginning so that they will have a definite focus for their initial activities. In learning about discussions, children will need guidance on where to begin. Figure 4.21 suggests several sources where the appropriate information may be found and encourages children to note down points relevant to their area of research. It also draws attention to the fact that in a discussion, each argument needs to be backed up with evidence in order to give it weight and credibility. However, with very young children, the frame, 'Information retrieval' (Figure 4.21), could be used simply as a means of directing their research and to highlight the fact that arguments may be supported by information gathered from a variety of sources. Initially it may be easier for them to write down ideas within the discrete columns without focusing on the evidence. The teacher's role is to make this explicit to children through modelling and by examining a range of examples.

There are basically two structures which can be used for writing a discussion. The more simple and widely used one requires children to present all of the arguments for an issue balanced by the arguments against. A more challenging and complex model requires the juxtaposition of points for and against which are presented consecutively.

Figure 4.22 offers a simple frame in which children, supported by sentence starters, are enabled to formulate a simple discussion. In Figure 4.23 the opening sentence can be written either as a question or a statement, for example 'Does violence on television make for a more violent society?' or 'Violence on television promotes violence in society.' It emphasises the

Discussion

Information retrieval

I am researching:

	Media (TV/video)	ICT (CD ROM/ Internet)	What I know	What my friends know	Information books
Key point					
Evidence					
Key point					
Evidence					
Key point					
Evidence					

Figure 4.21 Non-fiction – Discussion 1

Discussion

We are discussing whether

This may be a good thing because	This may be a bad thing because	Notes
•	•	
•	•	
•	•	
•	•	
•	•	

But I think

because

Figure 4.22 Non-fiction – Discussion 2

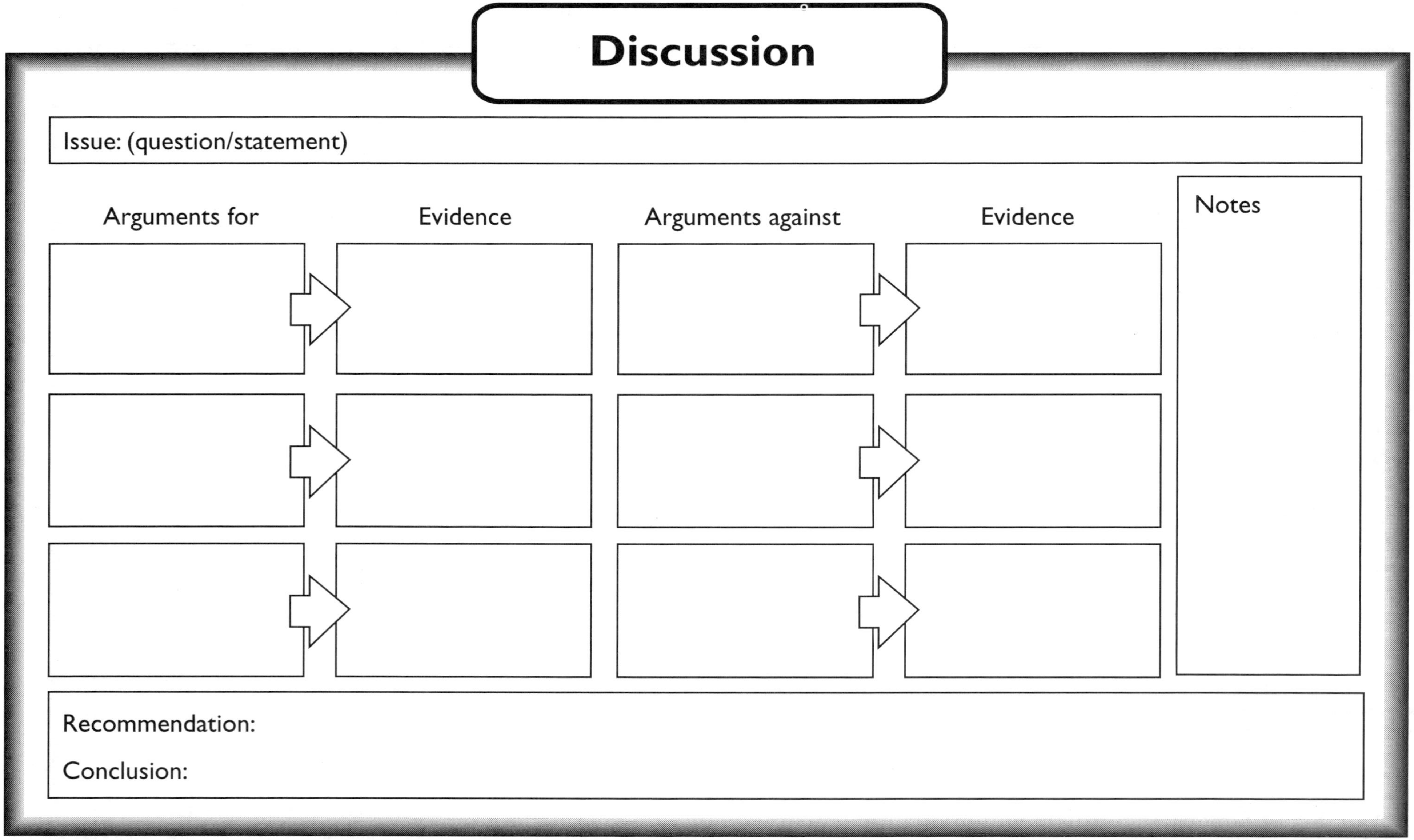

Discussion

Issue: (question/statement)

Arguments for

Evidence

Arguments against

Evidence

Notes

Recommendation:

Conclusion:

Figure 4.23 Non-fiction – Discussion 3

importance of evidence to back up each point and draws attention to the need for rounding the information off into reasoned recommendations and conclusions. The more complex structure for the discussion genre is illustrated by Figure 4.24. It moves children on a stage as it invites them to consider each argument which is immediately balanced by a counter argument.

Reflection

Children will have gained new knowledge and skills in writing these non-fiction genres and it is important that this knowledge is reflected upon and consolidated. In the first chapter, 'Reflecting', (Figure 1.14), presents questions which are relevant to any genre. These will enable children to consider the whole process of text construction in which they have engaged and the final question, 'How do you feel about the finished result?' could form the basis of a useful dialogue between teacher and child so developing the teaching and learning process further. In this way, key features of the genre can be reinforced and appropriate targets set.

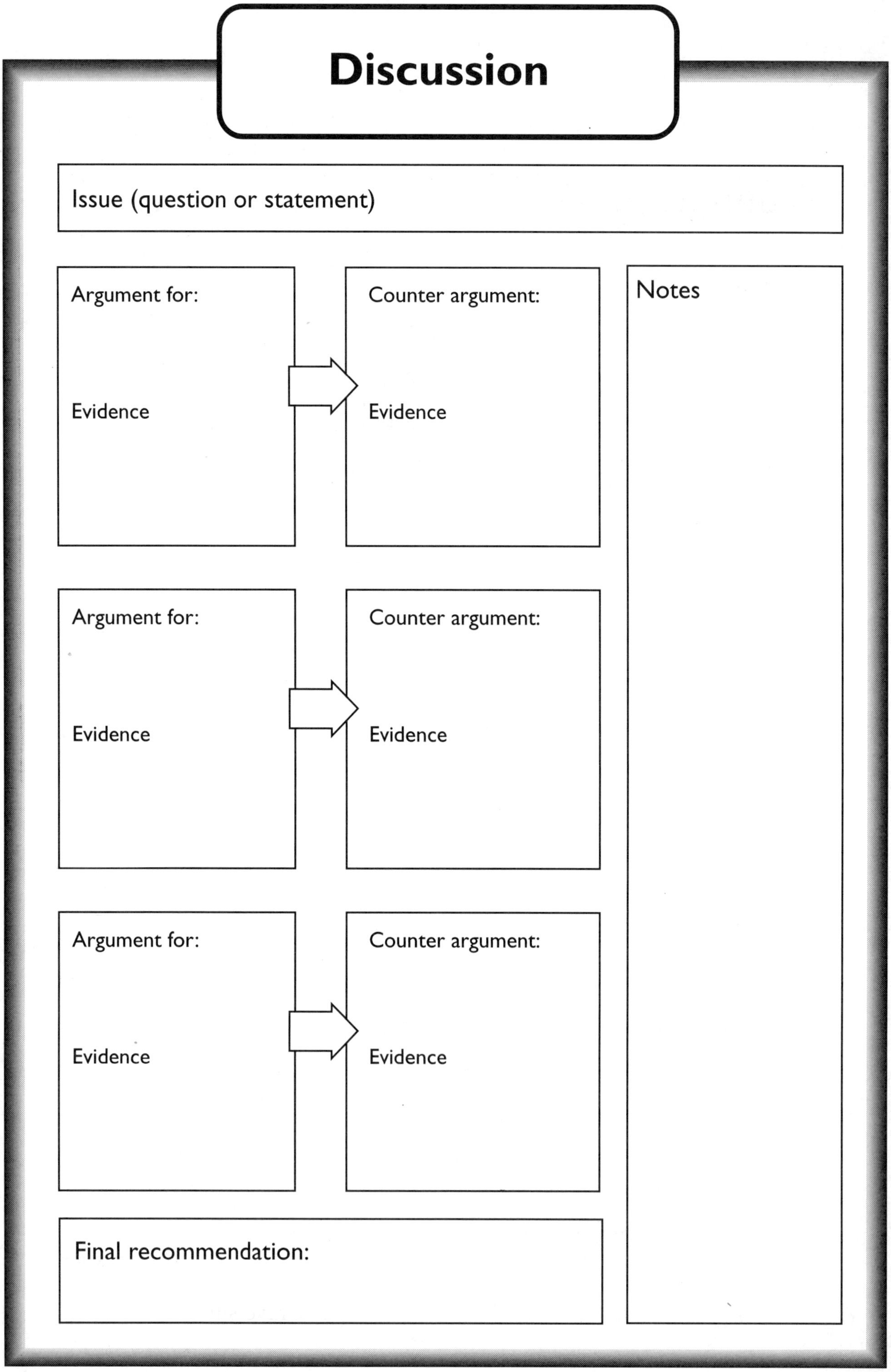

Discussion

Issue (question or statement)

Argument for:	Counter argument:	Notes
Evidence	Evidence	

Argument for:	Counter argument:
Evidence	Evidence

Argument for:	Counter argument:
Evidence	Evidence

Final recommendation:

Figure 4.24 Non-fiction – Discussion 4

Bibliography

Browne, A. (1996) *Developing Language and Literacy 3–8*. London: Paul Chapman Publishing.

Carter, D. (2000) *Teaching Fiction in the Primary School: Classroom approaches to narrative*. London: David Fulton Publishers.

Czerniewska, P. (1992) *Learning about Writing*. Oxford: Blackwell.

DfEE (1998) *The National Literacy Strategy: Framework for Teaching*. London: HMSO.

DfEE (1999) *The National Curriculum: Handbook for Primary Teachers in England*. London: HMSO.

DfEE (2000) *The National Literacy Strategy: Grammar for Writing*. London: HMSO.

Fisher, R. and Williams, M. (eds) (2000) *Unlocking Literacy. A Guide for Teachers*. London: David Fulton Publishers.

Graham, J. and Kelly, A. (1998) *Writing under Control: Teaching Writing in the Primary School*. London: David Fulton Publishers.

Graves, D. (1983) *Writing: Teachers and Children at Work*. London: Heinemann.

Hoey, M. (1983) *On the Surface of Discourse*. London: Allen and Unwin.

Lewis, M. and Wray, D. (1995) *Developing Children's Non-Fiction Writing: Working with Frames*. Scholastic.

Longacre, R. (1976) *An Anatomy of Speech Notions*. Lisse: Peter De Riddes.

Marsh, J. and Hallet, E. (ed.) (1999) *Desirable Literacies: Approaches to language and literacy in the early years*. London: Paul Chapman Publishing.

OFSTED (1999) *The National Literacy Strategy: An evaluation of the first year of the National Literacy Strategy*. London: HMSO.

OFSTED (1999) *An Evaluation of the First Year of the National Literacy Strategy*, 82, p. 15. London: HMSO.

OFSTED (1999) *Standards in English*. London: HMSO, p. 2., p. 3.

Parker, S. (1993) *The Craft of Writing*. London: Paul Chapman Publishing.

Sedgwick, F. (1997) *Read my Mind: Young children, poetry and learning*. London: Routledge.

Smith, F. (1982) *Writing and the Writer*. London: Heinemann.

Thomas, H. (1998) *Reading and Responding to Fiction: Classroom strategies for developing literacy*. Scholastic Limited.

Wyse, D. (1998) *Primary Writing*. Buckingham: Open University Press.

Index

advertisements 73
annotating 54
audience 2, 9, 27, 54, 55, 73
autobiography 55
autonomy 2, 14, 41

ballad 40
biography 55
brainstorming 5, 23, 27, 41, 55, 61

character 23, 27, 39
chronological 5, 56
collaboration 55
collaborative writing 9, 46, 54
connectives 9, 56
crafting 2, 5, 23, 40, 41, 54

decision making 2, 40, 41, 46
diaries 17, 55
dictionaries 9
differentiation 14, 27, 56
drafting 2, 9, 14, 46

empowerment 40, 54

flow diagrams 5, 9
form 9, 46
free verse 40

genre 14, 23, 40, 53, 54–56, 70
glossary 70
grammar 5, 35, 41, 54, 55, 70

handwriting 17, 50

ICT 14, 17
independence 19, 23, 55
information retrieval 54, 55, 79
interventions, teacher 5

journals 17

letters 17

matching (poetry) 46
modelling 2, 5, 14, 35, 46, 54, 55

narrative voice 23, 39
narrator 35
National Curriculum 2, 22, 53
National Literacy Strategy (NLS) 2, 22, 53, 54
newspaper reports 55
non-chronological 5
non-fiction texts
  discussion 79, 84
  explanation 70, 73
  instructional/
    procedural 61, 70
  non-chronological
    reports 56, 61
  persuasion 73
  recount 55–56
note-taking 54

organising orientation 56

partnership 17
planning 2, 5, 27
point of view 79
presenting 2, 17, 50

proof-reading 2, 46
publishing 17
punctuation 5, 9, 46
purpose 2, 9, 54, 55, 73

reading 2
recipes 61
reflecting 9, 17, 19, 35, 50, 84
re-orientation 56
responding 14
response partner 9, 14, 46, 55, 70, 73
revising 2, 46

scaffolding 5, 23
sentence construction 19, 55
senses 35
sequencing 27
setting 35, 39
shaping (poetry) 41, 46
shared reading 2
sonnet 46
spell checks 14
spelling 5, 9, 46

target, conference 19
target setting 19, 84
tone 73
transcription 9, 46

verbs 70
vocabulary 9, 19, 27 54, 55, 56
voice 73

word-processing 17, 50